© Aladdin Books Ltd 2001

Designed and produced by
Aladdin Books Ltd
28 Percy Street
London W1P 0LD

*First published in
Great Britain in 2001 by*
Franklin Watts
96 Leonard Street
London EC2A 4XD

ISBN 0 7496 4168 1

*A catalogue record for this
book is available from the
British Library.*

Printed in Belgium

Editor
Bibby Whittaker

Literacy Consultant
Jackie Holderness
Westminster Institute of Education,
Oxford Brookes University

Design
Flick, Book Design and Graphics

Picture Research
Brian Hunter Smart

Illustration
Mary Lonsdale for SGA

Picture Credits
Abbreviations: t – top, m – middle,
b – bottom, r – right, l – left, c –
centre. All photographs supplied by
Select Pictures except for Cover,
2tl, 9 — Corbis. 7 — Corbis/Royalty
Free. 10tl, 13, 14b, 22tr, 23tl,
23ml — Stockbyte. 12tl — Digital
Stock. 15 — E & D Hosking/FLPA-
Images of Nature. 16tr — Roger
Vlitos. 17 — John Deere.
19 — Michael Howard Homes.

READING ABOUT
Shapes

By Jim Pipe

Aladdin/Watts
London • Sydney

Shapes

Amy and Jon are at the beach.

What shapes can they see?

Jon can see round shapes.
Amy can see triangles.

The shells on the sand are
all kinds of shapes.

Square

What shape is Amy's net?

Amy's net is square, like squares on a chess board. A square has straight sides. Every side is the same length.

These bricks have six sides.

Each side is a square.

This shape is called a cube.

Rectangle

What shape is Amy's towel?

It is a rectangle, like a book. It has two short sides and two long sides. All its corners are the same.

A kite has four sides, too.
Its corners are not all the
same, so it is not a rectangle!

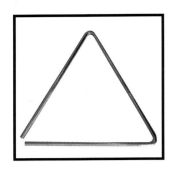

Triangle

What shape is that sail?

It is a triangle. A triangle has three straight sides.

Can you see any other triangles?

These pyramids have walls that are very big triangles.

 # Round

What shape is Amy's board?

It is round. It does not have corners like a square.

Some shapes are round.

Some shapes have straight sides.

What shape is an ice cream cone?

Circle

What shape is Jon's big ring?

It is a round shape, called a circle.

It rolls along like a wheel.

A ball is round all over.

Push it left, push it right.

Push it forward, push it back.

A ball can roll everywhere!

Animal shapes

Amy sees an animal in the water.

What shape is it?

It has five points like a star.

It is a starfish!

This snake has
shapes on its skin.

Diamond

These shapes are called diamonds.
A diamond has four sides.

Machine shapes

What shapes can you find on Jon's diggers?

There are circles, triangles, rectangles and squares!

Some shapes are good for digging.
Some shapes are good for pushing.

What shapes can
you find on a
bicycle or tractor?

Adding shapes

You can add shapes to make a new shape. What shapes does Amy use in her sand picture?

A house can be many shapes.

Some parts look like triangles.

Some parts look like rectangles.

What shapes are on this house?

Lots of shapes

You can make lots of shapes with sand.

Look at Amy and Jon's
big sandcastle!

What shapes can
you see?

Here are some words about shape.

Straight

Round

Square

Circle

Triangle

Rectangle

22

What shape are these things?

Ball

Shells

Starfish

Digger

Kite

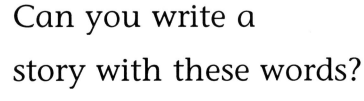

Can you write a
story with these words?

23

Do you know?

You can make a triangle from a paper square. Fold it in half!

Square

Triangle

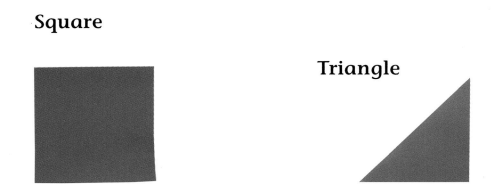

You can even fold it into a plane!

Plane